W9-AMC-064

LATINOS IN BASEBALL

Bobby Bonilla

John A. Torres

Mitchell Lane Publishers, Inc.
P.O. Box 200
Childs, MD 21916-0200

LATINOS IN BASEBALL

Tino Martinez	**Bobby Bonilla**	Roberto Alomar	Pedro Martinez
Moises Alou	Sammy Sosa	Ivan Rodriguez	Carlos Baerga
Ramon Martinez	Alex Rodriguez	Vinny Castilla	Mariano Rivera

Library of Congress Cataloging-in-Publication Data

Torres, John Albert.
     Bobby Bonilla / John A. Torres.
        p. cm. — (Latinos in baseball)
     Includes index.
     Summary: Describes the childhood and baseball career of the superstar who has played for six teams, including the Pittsburgh Pirates and the New York Mets.
     ISBN 1-883845-83-1 (lib. bdg.)
     1. Bonilla, Bobby, 1963- —Juvenile literature. 2. Baseball players—United States—Biography—Juvenlle literature. [1. Bonilla, Bobby, 1963- . 2. Baseball players. 3. Hispanic Americans—Biography.] I. Title. II. Series.
GV865.B65T67 1999
96.357'092—dc21
[B]
     98-48050
     CIP
     AC

About the Author: John A. Torres is a newspaper reporter for the Poughkeepsie Journal in New York. He has written eleven sports biographies, including *Greg Maddux* (Lerner), *Hakeem Olajuwon* (Enslow), and *Darryl Strawberry* (Enslow). He lives in Fishkill, New York with his wife and two children. When not writing, John likes to spend his time fishing, coaching Little League baseball, and spending time with his family.

Photo Credits: cover: Bill Hickey/Allsport; pp. 4, 6, 7, 9 © 1998 Florida Marlins/Denis Bancroft; p. 12 © 1998 L.A. Dodgers/Juan Ocampo; p. 25 UPI/Corbis-Bettmann; pp. 35, 37 Otto Greule Jr./Allsport; p. 44 Reuters/Corbis-Bettmann; pp. 50, 52 © 1996 Jerry Wachter; p. 55 © 1998 Florida Marlins/Denis Bancroft; pp. 57, 58, 59 © 1998 L. A. Dodgers/Juan Ocampo; p. 61 John Swart/Allsport.

Acknowledgments: This story has been thoroughly researched and checked for accuracy. To the best of our knowledge, it represents a true story.

TABLE OF CONTENTS

Bobby Bonilla has played for many teams in his major-league career, including one season with the world champion Florida Marlins.

CHAPTER ONE
Good Guy Wins Championship

It was a hot and muggy night and the fans were quiet and uncomfortable. Things did not look good. The hometown Florida Marlins were losing 2-0 and were only nine outs away from losing the 1997 World Series to the Cleveland Indians. It was the deciding seventh game. Whichever team won this game would go home the world champion.

Bobby Bonilla wandered behind home plate as he waited for his turn to bat. He had been mired in a horrendous 4-for-26 slump in the Series. The fans were behind him, though. They knew that Bobby had a severely strained hamstring and was playing through a lot of pain.

Bobby recognized an old-time pitcher watching the game from behind home plate. It was Joe Black, who had been a great pitcher for the old Brooklyn Dodgers. Bobby approached him, hoping that he could give him a tip, anything to help him get out of his slump.

"It looks like you are standing too close to home plate, Bobby," he said. "Why don't you back off the plate a little bit."

Bobby took his advice. He stepped back from the plate and dug in. He straightened his bat out over the plate, took a few quick practice swings, and stared at the pitcher. He then proceeded to blast a home run deep over the right-field fence. The advice had been valuable, and now the Marlins were only one run behind. The fans gave Bobby a standing ovation.

The Marlins proceeded to tie the game in the bottom of the ninth and forced extra innings. The fans were in a frenzy. The eleventh inning rolled around and

In Game 7 of the 1997 World Series against the Cleveland Indians, Bobby Bonilla blasted a home run deep over the right field fence to bring the Marlins within one run of a tie game.

the leadoff batter for Florida was Bobby. He singled sharply and represented the winning run. Bobby moved to third on another base hit. The fans stood and cheered his effort. They knew his injury was bothering him but he still ran his hardest. After a walk loaded the bases, Marlin youngster Edgar Renteria came to bat. There

Bobby Bonilla (24) and teammate Moises Alou (18) both played one season for the Florida Marlins—the year they won the World Series.

were two outs. Edgar singled up the middle, Bobby scored, and the Florida Marlins were the World Champions. The fans went wild.

Bobby had dreamed of this moment his entire life. As a child he would swing his baseball bat in his Bronx apartment and pretend to be a major-leaguer. The dream would always end the same: with Bobby hitting a home run and winning the World Series.

Bobby hugged his manager and old friend, Jim Leyland, and cried. This was Bobby's 12th season and his fifth big-league team. He was finally a champion. But it had not been easy.

The Marlins had overcome incredible odds to even make it to the Series. They finished the season with the National League East's second-best record. That was good enough to clinch a wild-card berth in the major-league playoffs behind the first-place Atlanta Braves. They faced off against the tough San Francisco Giants and swept them easily three games to zero in the best-of-five series in the first round of the playoffs. Then they had to face the defending National League champions, the Braves, and their tough pitching staff.

Bobby and his teammates played well. They defeated Atlanta four games to two with Bobby and tough-hitting teammate Gary Sheffield leading the way. In fact, Bobby drove in three runs in the final game of the series to clinch the pennant and defeat Atlanta 7-4. He played even though he had earlier aggravated a hamstring injury that nearly forced him from the Series.

Bobby and teammates celebrated their world championship.

After the Marlins clinched the pennant, Bobby met Leyland at home plate and the two men hugged.

"I love you, Bobby," Leyland said. "We're going to the World Series."

"The World Series," Bobby answered. "I can't believe I'm even saying those words."

Bobby's injury was severe. Leyland asked him if he would be able to play in the World Series.

"It took me twelve and a half years to get here and I'm not going to miss it," Bobby vowed.

In fact, the two old friends had come a long way, together and separately. Leyland and Bobby had been together for six years when Bobby played for the Pittsburgh Pirates and Leyland was his manager. The Pirates had some great teams in the early 1990s with Bobby, Andy Van Slyke, and Barry Bonds terrorizing National League pitchers. But they had always seemed to come up just short and never made it to the World Series.

Eventually the team was broken up. Barry signed with the San Francisco Giants and Bobby returned home to play for his hometown team, the New York Mets. Leyland stayed and managed some terrible Pirates teams until he decided to go to South Florida and become the Marlins manager.

Leyland saw many changes in Bobby over the years. An angry and often injured Bonilla had replaced the smiling, happy player he once knew. When Bobby signed as a free agent with Florida before the 1997 season, Leyland was hoping that the old Bobby would return.

Bobby had earned the reputation as being a surly and even a selfish player. In New York, he had even threatened a local sportswriter. In Baltimore, he feuded with manager Davey Johnson about switching positions. When Bobby showed up in Florida, the local media did not know what to expect. Leyland even joked about a new sheriff being in town. But Bobby shocked them.

Bobby had returned to his old self. He played the game to have fun. He was friendly to the media and even gave a lot of his time to local charities. He was a nice guy to be around, and many of his teammates regarded him as the team leader.

Bobby was comfortable playing in Florida. He was also comfortable playing for his old manager and friend again. He was so cooperative, in fact, that the sportswriters who covered the team voted to award him the Charlie Hough Good Guy Award. This award is given annually to a local southern Florida athlete who is cooperative with the media.

Bobby was very proud of the award. He even joked that the sportswriters in New York would never believe it. Bobby had had a rough time with the New York writers while he was a member of the Mets.

He had come a long way and traveled a strange road. It started in the Bronx, moved to Europe, Pittsburgh, Chicago, back to Pittsburgh, home to New York, to Baltimore, to Miami, to Los Angeles, and then home one more time to New York. But Bobby Bonilla proved that good guys can win. Nice guys can finish first.

For the 1998 baseball season, Bobby played for the Los Angeles Dodgers.

CHAPTER 2
Growing Up

Roberto Martin Antonio Bonilla was born on February 23, 1963, in the Bronx, New York. His parents called him Bobby or Robert. His father, Roberto, was born in New York City to Cuban and Puerto Rican parents. Since he was born in New York, he spoke English very well. But he also spoke Spanish, and he kept very close to his roots.

Bobby's mother, Regina, was born in Puerto Rico. She moved to New York when she was a young woman.

Puerto Rico is an island about 1,000 miles south of the United States. Spanish is spoken on the island, and *Puerto Rico* is Spanish for "rich port." Puerto Rico is an American commonwealth, which means it is the property of the United States. All of the people in Puerto Rico are U.S. citizens.

Bobby's parents moved a lot when he was very young because the south Bronx, where they lived, was becoming a dangerous neighborhood. As each block or part of the neighborhood changed into a crime zone, Roberto and Regina packed their things and moved to another part. They tried to stay one step ahead of the crime.

"You worried about your children's safety," said Regina. "It was a ghetto—you didn't walk on the street at night."

Regina gave birth to Bobby's twin sisters about a year after he was born. They were named Milagros and Socorro.

The family lived for a while on the top floor of a five-story apartment building on Trinity Avenue, behind the Jackson Avenue Projects. The area was mainly black and Hispanic.

Roberto and Regina tried to get Bobby and his sisters involved in sports from a very young age. They felt it would be a good way to keep them off the streets and away from the gangs and the drugs.

Roberto was an electrician. He would sometimes take Bobby to work with him. Bobby enjoyed watching his father connect wires and give people light, but he also knew he did not want to become an electrician when he got older. He did not like how hard his father had to work. He also did not like it when he saw his father get thrown off a ladder by an electrical shock. But still, Bobby admired his dad. He would often say that his father was his hero.

Bobby would watch baseball games on television with his father and his grandfather. He grew to love sports. His favorites were baseball, basketball, and football, but he was really fascinated by the strategies of baseball.

If Bobby knew he did not want to become an electrician at that young age, he also knew one other thing: he did not want to become a drug addict.

Drugs had infested the neighborhood where Bobby lived. He saw a lot of kids get hooked and their lives ruined because of drugs. Sometimes he was afraid to leave his apartment. He would look through the peephole and sometimes see people injecting drugs such as heroin in the hallway right outside his door.

"It made me realize that was not where I wanted my life to lead," Bobby said.

It took a strong person not to get involved with drugs when they seemed to be all around. But Bobby had a lot of help. Not only was his father a good role model for him, his mother was, too.

Regina worked at nearby Lincoln Hospital. She also attended night classes at Columbia University to get a master's degree in social work. She showed Bobby that with hard work and education, he could go places.

Meanwhile, Bobby continued to show his love of sports. Besides playing baseball, basketball, and football, he also played a lot of inner-city games. His favorites were stickball, which is like baseball but played with a broom handle for a bat and a soft rubber ball, and spongeball, which uses a ball that is a combination handball and baseball. After slapping the bounce-pitched ball with an open hand, the player ran around the bases to try to score runs.

During the warm months of the year, Bobby could be found playing baseball at Crotona Park, St. Mary's Park, or Macombs Dam Park. Bobby grew up a Yankee fan, but he also liked the hometown Mets. He once went to a Mets game and caught a foul ball that had gone into the stands. After playing sports all day, Bobby would rush home and watch sports highlights on television. His favorite announcer was Warner Wolf. He would imitate how Wolf would say "Swoosh!" and "Let's go to the videotape!"

When Bobby was eight years old, his brother, Javier, was born. The happiness brought by the new addition to the family was short-lived, however. Just a few months later, Bobby's parents got divorced.

Even though Bobby's father was not living with them, he remained an important part of his children's lives. He would still spend a lot of time with them and would honk his horn outside their apartment building at night to make sure everybody was safe and sound. He remained active in their lives.

Bobby was an average student and was well liked. He attended the public schools in the area. From kindergarten through the sixth grade, Bobby attended Public School 77. His favorite subject was art. He won an art contest once; the prize was Mets tickets.

At P.S. 77, Bobby was enrolled in a program called Follow Through. This was a federally funded program designed to help underprivileged kids excel in school. It encouraged them, through incentives, not to drop out of school and to stay off drugs. Many poor neighborhoods have high dropout rates.

Bobby later attended Intermediate School 162. He also played Little League baseball from age nine through 12. Bobby was known as being an honest kid who was always smiling. He was very popular and had a lot of friends.

When Bobby started playing Little League, he realized that he was pretty good at baseball. He started taking his bat everywhere he went. After a while he even started sleeping with it. Bobby and his bat seemed inseparable. He spent every spare minute practicing his swing. At first people thought he was a troublemaker because of his ever-present bat.

One night when he could not sleep, Bobby climbed out of bed and started swinging. Soon it became a ritual. Bobby would pretend he was a Yankee or a Met and that he was hitting home runs in the seventh game of the World Series. The only problem was that Bobby shared a room with Javier, who had to be careful not to get hit.

"It was a nightmare; he almost hit me a couple of times," Javier said.

When it was time for high school, Bobby decided he wanted to go to a vocational school to learn to be an automobile mechanic. He knew it was good to have a solid trade or skill. Bobby would have liked to one day open his own garage. But Bobby's mother had different ideas. She wanted her son to aspire to something more. She hoped that he could get into the medical field.

She enrolled Bobby in Lehman High School, which was in a different and safer neighborhood. It was not easy for Bobby. It would take him more than an hour and two buses to get to school.

But Bobby sacrificed, and it changed his life forever.

CHAPTER 3
High-School Superstar

Bobby was only an average student at Lehman High School, but his big smile and easygoing personality made him very popular. The school was racially mixed, and Bobby made a lot of friends. He had only really been exposed to black and Hispanic kids, but he was able to fit in with just about everyone at Lehman.

Besides his studies, Bobby had only one thing on his mind: baseball. He had pretty much stopped playing other sports and concentrated on baseball all year round. He wanted to try out for Lehman's baseball team, but he knew it would be tough. After gaining enough courage, he went to a tryout.

Coach Joe Levine liked Bobby from the first minute he saw him. He liked his attitude, and he also liked his raw potential. Bobby was fast and strong, but he needed a lot of work on his fundamentals and his grace. He was a little clumsy on the field.

Bobby tried out for almost every position. There was one spot left on the team, and Levine decided to give it to Bobby. The coach needed a versatile player, someone who could and was willing to play any position.

Shortly after making the baseball team, Bobby did something else that would change his life forever:

he met Millie Quinones. He met her in the school cafeteria, and soon they became boyfriend and girlfriend.

Bobby did not play much baseball as a high-school freshman, but he was still proud to have made the team and he still practiced hard. He also always carried that baseball bat wherever he went.

Coach Levine took an active part in Bobby's high-school experience. He made sure that Bobby understood how important it was to be on time for his classes and to do his schoolwork. He also stressed that regardless of the amount of playing time he received, he must always practice his hardest.

Bobby liked high school, and he thought about going to college to become a filmmaker. He loved the freedom that filmmakers had and how they were able to transform their vision to the big screen. He thought it might be a good career for him.

When Bobby was 15, the New York Mets held an open tryout. They were trying to find local, unsigned talent. Bobby did not really believe he could make the Mets, but he thought it would be fun to try. The Mets were not interested in Bobby, but he came home with a souvenir for Millie. He had put some of the infield dirt from Shea Stadium into a little jewelry box for her. He thought that would be his only connection to the major leagues.

As a sophomore at Lehman, Bobby began to show his worth on the team. He became the team's most versatile player. He played outfield, second base, shortstop, and even catcher. One day during batting practice, Bobby asked Coach Levine if he could try his hand at switch-hitting. He thought it would make him more valuable to the team. A switch-hitter bats from both sides of the plate, batting right-handed against left-handed pitchers and left-handed against right-handed pitchers. Up until that point, Bobby had strictly been a right-handed batter.

Coach Levine was amazed at how well Bobby did and told him that from then on he was a switch-hitter.

Bobby was very popular in high school. Everyone knew Bobby by his big smile and his upbeat personality. He had a lot of friends.

During his junior and senior seasons at Lehman, Bobby hit near .500, meaning that he reached base safely nearly half the time he batted. More importantly for Coach Levine, Bobby became a team leader. He was known for his team spirit and for not letting his teammates down. He didn't worry about his own statistics; he only cared about his team's winning.

By June of his senior year, Bobby was wondering if any major-league teams would draft him in the annual amateur draft. June came and went, and Bobby was not chosen. Even though he was disappointed, he decided to go to college in the fall. Coach Levine helped Bobby to go to the New York Technical Institute. Bobby would have a chance to get an education and play baseball at the same time. If he did well, maybe a baseball team would draft him then. Bobby still held on to a little hope that one day he would be swinging his bat for a major-league baseball team.

A few weeks before graduation, Coach Levine heard about a great opportunity for Bobby. An amateur American baseball team was being started up to play in an international tournament. The goal of the program was to expose and bring baseball to countries where it was not played. The hope was that maybe it would catch on and become a world sport like basketball or soccer.

Coach Levine signed Bobby up for the program. Then there was only one obstacle left: Bobby could not afford the cost of the airline ticket to Europe. Coach Levine organized an impromptu drive to get Bobby the money. Coffee cans were placed in just about every classroom, and students were urged to donate whatever change they could so that Bobby could buy the ticket.

The collection was known as the Bobby Fund. Students and teachers filled the cans daily, and soon Bobby had the $1,500 he needed for the trip. His popularity had paid off in a way he had never imagined. His classmates liked him so much that they paid for him to go to Europe. He was set for the trip that would take him to Denmark, Sweden, and Finland.

It was Bobby's good fortune that one of his teammates was another high-school graduate by the name of Jim Thrift. Jim's father, Syd Thrift, was a front-office employee and future general manager of the Pittsburgh Pirates. Syd Thrift accompanied the team to watch his son play and to conduct baseball clinics for children in the foreign countries.

After watching the team practice, Syd Thrift was surprised that Bobby had never been drafted. He had never even heard of Bobby. Here was an 18-year-old who had size, power, speed, and a good arm. Thrift decided to keep an eye on Bobby throughout the tournament.

The team started out slowly, as the players seemed to suffer from a team-wide batting slump. One night Bobby slept with a famous hitting book under his pillow. The next day he cracked a home run and belted out a few other hits. Soon every one of his teammates was asking to borrow the book. They wanted to sleep with it, too!

By the end of the tournament, Bobby had once again established himself as a team leader and as an all-around great guy. And Syd Thrift had made up his mind that Bobby was major-league material. He wanted to offer him a contract.

Coach Levine was very happy for Bobby. He knew that Bobby had what it took. "He had the enjoyment of playing—of being the best you can be. Every kid dreams of being a major-leaguer. Some kids screw up their lives; Bobby didn't," Levine said.

Bobby was not a major-leaguer yet. If he were to make it, he had a long way to go. But now he was one step closer. He signed a $10,000 contract and became a professional baseball player.

Bobby was lucky to become part of the Pittsburgh Pirates family. The Pirates were known as a patient organization. They liked to foster young talent, and they were also very patient and understanding of the needs of Hispanic ballplayers.

Bobby reported to Bradenton, Florida, where he would play in the Florida Gulf Coast League. This was the lowest-level minor-league team that the Pirates had. Bobby worked out for three hours in the hot Florida sun every morning and then again in the afternoon. He was very homesick. He spent every free moment talking on the phone with Millie, who was still in New York. Bobby made $650 a month and spent $200 on his phone bill.

Bobby appeared in only 22 games, but he was still able to prove his versatility. He played first base, catcher, and third base. He managed 15 hits in 69 at-bats for a .217 batting average.

Bobby became depressed about being away from home. He began to gain weight, causing the Pirates to monitor his eating habits. He liked to eat sweets, which he had to stop doing. He knew that it would be tough to make the major leagues, so he began to make alternative plans just in case. In the off-season, he enrolled at New York Technical Institute to study filmmaking. His favorite director was Steven Spielberg. Bobby liked how his movies combined fantasy and action. His favorite movies were *Raiders of the Lost Ark* and *E.T. The Extra-Terrestrial*, both Spielberg films.

"Spielberg has the kind of imagination I'd like to have," Bobby said.

After only one semester, Bobby went back to Florida. This was a very important moment in Bobby's life. It was time to decide whether baseball or movies would be his future. It looked like baseball had won.

Bobby has always felt lucky that he started his baseball career with the Pittsburgh Pirates. The team liked to foster young talent and they were a patient organization.

CHAPTER 4
The Minor Leagues

Bobby reported to Bradenton, Florida, again for the next season. He was determined to show that he belonged with the other prospects. He had slimmed down a bit and had also gotten a lot stronger.

The added strength showed when Bobby came to bat. In only 47 games, Bobby belted 15 home runs and drove in 26 runs. He still hit only .228, but officials in the Pirates organization were not worried. They envisioned Bobby as a major-league switch-hitting power hitter within a few years.

Scouts for other teams began to take notice of Bobby. They liked his raw skills, but they all agreed that he needed a lot of work. Bobby heard the talk. He wanted to escape life in the Bronx. He decided it was time to work even harder, so he spent a lot of the winter playing in Puerto Rico to make sure that he stayed in good game shape.

The hard work paid off, and Bobby was promoted to Alexandria, Virginia to their Class A team. He proved that he was indeed a power hitter, and he was able to raise his batting average up to respectability. Bobby hit 11 home runs with 59 RBIs. He also batted .256.

By 1984, Bobby found himself one step closer to the major leagues. The Pirates promoted him again to their Nashua team in New Hampshire. This was Pittsburgh's AA team. There was only one more level of the minor leagues between Bobby and the majors.

In Nashua it was decided that Bobby was best suited for the outfield. Up until that point he had sort of filled in at a lot of positions. That season he played 131 games in the outfield and two games at first base. It made him comfortable to play just one position. He led the team with 11 round-trippers, or home runs. He also tied for the team lead with 71 RBIs. The Pirates were so impressed with Bobby's progress that they told him to report to their major-league spring training the following season. They wanted to give Bobby a shot at making their major-league club.

Bobby worked hard all winter and showed up to spring training in Florida in the best shape of his life. He hustled and tried his best to show the Pirates that he was serious about becoming a major-league player. The Pirates planned to send him to their AAA team in Hawaii for a few months before calling him up for good. But it was Bobby's own hustle and hard play that almost ruined his career.

On March 22, 1985, the Pirates were playing a spring training exhibition game against the Kansas City Royals. Bobby was playing right field. There was a short pop fly into shallow right field. Bobby came in as hard as he could. Pittsburgh's second baseman, Bip Roberts, ran out toward the outfield as fast as he could. The ball dropped between the two players, but not before they collided with each other at full speed. Bobby fell to the ground in excruciating pain. His leg was broken.

Many people thought that Bobby's career was over. It is very hard to completely recover from such a severe leg injury. Now Bobby was more determined than ever. He had come so close to making it to the major leagues. He had tasted it. He wanted to be there, so he worked like he never had before.

"It could definitely have been a career-threatening injury, but nobody worked harder than Bobby did," said Hall of Fame Pirate slugger Willie "Pops" Stargell, who is still very involved with the Pirates.

Bobby was not expected to return to the baseball field for at least a year. But he worked extremely hard and made it back in only four months. He reported to Pittsburgh's Prince William team in the Class A Carolina League and played himself back into shape there. It was in Prince William that he met another Pirate prospect: Barry Bonds. Bonds is the son of former Yankees and Giants superstar Bobby Bonds. Bobby Bonilla and Barry Bonds became good friends. They were the future of the Pirates organization.

Bobby played in the team's final 39 games that season and batted .262 with three homers and 11 RBIs. After the season, he chose to go to Puerto Rico and play winter ball. He wanted to prove to the Pirates that he was a hard worker and that he was ready for the pros.

Bobby played hard in Puerto Rico and was having a great time, except for one thing. Something was missing in his life: Millie. He spent every free minute talking to her on the phone. He was so broke that he jokingly told Millie it would be cheaper if they got married. Then he realized that he loved her more than anything and did want to marry her. She caught the next plane to Puerto Rico, and Bobby borrowed a few dollars from his friend and teammate Juan Agosto to buy the marriage license. Bobby and Millie became husband and wife.

Now the only thing left was the major leagues. Bobby was no longer homesick. He played very well in Puerto Rico, and many major-league teams sent their scouts to watch this virtually unknown player named Bobby Bonilla.

In baseball, every team is allowed to put its best 40 players on a protected roster during the off-season. The players who are not protected can be drafted by other teams in something called the Rule V draft. This means that another team can draft a player and keep him as long as he stays on the major-league team all season. If a team tried to return the player to the minor leagues, he would have to be offered back to his original team first.

The Pirates liked Bobby a lot and were counting on him to be a major-leaguer very soon. But they did not put him on their 40-man roster. The Pirates believed that other teams would not draft him because of his recently injured leg. They were wrong. Because Bobby played so well in Puerto Rico, many teams were interested in obtaining him.

The Chicago White Sox drafted Bobby in December of 1985. Bobby was filled with mixed emotions. The only organization he ever knew was the Pittsburgh Pirates. He felt lost without their support. On the other hand, being chosen in the Rule V draft meant something else. Bobby's dream would be coming true. He was going to the major leagues.

Syd Thrift, who had discovered and signed Bobby, had been recently named as the general manager for the Pirates. He could not believe that the Pirates had lost Bobby in the draft. "I was very, very disappointed to lose Bobby," Thrift said. He was determined to get him back.

Meanwhile Bobby was a member of the Chicago White Sox. He went to spring training and knew that he would get a lot of playing time between playing first base and third base.

When the season started, Bobby found himself in the opening-day lineup. He played first base in the game against the Detroit Tigers. Bobby had two singles in the game, his first major-league hits, and drove in a run to help the White Sox win the game 10-4.

A few weeks later, Bobby hit his first major-league home run. It came against Cleveland Indian knuckleball pitcher Phil Niekro. The Indians won the game 8-7, but Bobby was still proud to hit his first home run against a future Hall of Famer. Niekro won over 300 games in his career and was inducted to the Hall of Fame after he retired.

Midway through the season, Bobby was batting a decent .269 with two home runs and 26 runs batted in. He was showing himself to be a solid and versatile player. He did not show a lot of power, but many times younger players take a few years to develop their home-run strokes.

The White Sox were a contending team and were in desperate need of pitchers. Thrift had been keeping an eye on the situation all season long. He traded right-handed pitcher Jose DeLeon to Chicago for Bonilla. Bobby was back where he belonged. He was a Pittsburgh Pirate, again.

CHAPTER 5
Bobby the Pirate

Bobby Bonilla, or Bobby Bo as some fans call him, was again a member of the Pittsburgh Pirates. He felt comfortable; he was back home. Bobby played the rest of the season for the Pirates, but he only showed flashes of his brilliance. The Pirates coaches knew that Bobby could be a better player. They watched films of him playing and all agreed that there was one simple thing he had to do to improve his game. He had to become more aggressive.

By the spring of 1987, Bobby had developed into a main player for the Pirates. Manager Jim Leyland appreciated his versatility. In 1987, Bobby played two games at first base, eight in left field, 26 in right field, and 75 at third base. Leyland thought that Bobby could develop into an excellent third baseman.

Besides trying to turn Bobby into a more aggressive player, the Pittsburgh coaches also tinkered with his swing. They showed him that it was better to take a short, fast swing than a long, hard one. It would increase his bat speed and give him more power as well.

Bobby took their advice and soon was driving the ball to all parts of the field like he never had before.

That July, Bobby became the first Pirate ever to hit home runs from both sides of the plate in a single game. He belted a home run hitting right-handed against Los Angeles Dodger and ace pitcher Fernando Valenzuela. Later in the same game, while batting left-handed, Bobby smacked a homer off reliever Ken Howell.

Nine days later, Bobby made Pirate history again. While playing at Pittsburgh's Three Rivers Stadium, Bobby became only the seventh player to hit a home run into the upper deck of the stadium. It was a monstrous home run that probably would have traveled over 500 feet if the stands had not been there. The Pirates organization painted Bobby's uniform number, number 25, on the chair on which the ball had landed.

Bobby got hot in September and had an 11-game hitting streak. That means that he got at least one base hit a game for 11 straight games. He finished the season with a solid .300 batting average. He also belted 15 homers and drove in 77 runs. Another example of his incredible power was his 33 doubles. Bobby had what the scouts call extra-base-hit power. Bobby Bo was known as a very nice guy, and the players and fans began to like him a lot.

That's why the fans and players were shocked when Bobby lost his cool during the 1988 season. Bobby was called out on strikes by the umpire. Bobby thought that the pitch was clearly a ball. He started screaming at the umpire. The umpire threw Bobby out of the game.

The next day Bobby watched the play on videotape. The umpire had been right. The pitch was really a strike. Bobby went out onto the field and shook the umpire's hand and apologized.

Bobby was a rare professional athlete. As long as he was in the lineup, he did not care where he played on the field. His big hulking body made him more suited to play first base, but the Pirates needed him to play third. He worked hard on his agility and on his fielding. To improve his quickness and agility, he would jump on and off boxes. He would also jog in place between pitches while he was on the field. Even Phillie third baseman and Hall of Famer Mike Schmidt commented on how much Bobby had improved on his fielding.

Bobby was chosen the National League player of the month for April. He batted .341 with seven home runs. He won the honor again in May when he batted .344 with six more home runs.

Bobby was voted by the fans as the starting third baseman for the National League All-Star team. He was the first Pirate to start the All-Star Game since Dave Parker back in 1981. At the break he was batting .297 with 17 home runs and 57 RBIs.

Bobby made $230,000 for the 1988 season. It was the first time that he felt wealthy. Bobby, who had had to borrow money to buy a marriage license, splurged and bought himself a $53,000 car.

Once again Bobby hit two home runs from different sides of the plate in the same game. This time he victimized the Philadelphia Phillies. He belted a lefty home run against Kevin Gross and a righty homer against Jeff Calhoun. He finished the season with a .274 batting average, but he also hit 24 home runs and drove in 100 runs. Bobby said that the thing he was most proud of was the 100 runs batted in. Bobby was also named to the Sporting News Hillerich and Bradsby Silver Slugger Team.

As long as Bobby was in the line-up, he never really cared where he played on the field.

Bobby's good friend Barry Bonds had been called up to the majors in 1986. And like Bobby, he had been improving with every season. In 1988 Barry belted 24 home runs as well, and he and Bobby were the nucleus of a very solid batting order. The Pirates were starting to gain respect.

By 1989 the media and the fans were calling Bonilla and Bonds the Killer B's. The New York Mets had been the National League East's dominating team for the late 1980s, and the Pirates had been known as a laughingstock. But things were steadily changing. The Pirates began to assemble a solid team. They had a very good right fielder in Andy Van Slyke; Barry was in center; Bobby was at third base; and their talented pitching staff was anchored by right-handed ace Doug Drabek.

In 1989 Bobby was the team's best player. He led the Pirates in doubles, triples, home runs, and hits.

The manager of the Pittsburgh Pirates was Jim Leyland. He was known to be a patient man who was fair with his players. Leyland became close to Bobby, almost like a second father, and nurtured him. He had come to the Pirates in 1986 and was known as a player's manager.

In 1990 Bobby often played right field for the Bucs. (*Buc* is short for *buccaneer*, which is another word for *pirate*.) By midsummer, the Pirates were one of the best teams in all of baseball. Bobby and Barry were battling each other for the National League's MVP award. Bobby hit a grand slam on May 23 to win a game and then belted another one on August 23 to break open an important game against the Western Division's leading Cincinnati Reds.

On September 30, the Pirates clinched the National League Eastern Division title with a 2-0 victory over the St. Louis Cardinals. They were going to the playoffs for the first time in a long time. The players jumped up and down and danced on the field. Then they carried Leyland off the field on their shoulders.

In this 1990 photo below, Bobby waits his turn to bat.

Bobby had finished the season with a .280 batting average with 32 homers and 120 RBIs. He came in second place in the Most Valuable Player race to his teammate and friend, Barry Bonds. Barry had batted .301 with 33 home runs and 114 RBIs. Barry had also stolen 52 bases. Drabek was awarded the Cy Young Award for the league's best pitcher, and Leyland was named Manager of the Year.

The awards did not matter to Bobby. All he cared about was trying to beat the Cincinnati Reds in the playoffs and getting to the World Series.

Pittsburgh won the first game 4-3 when Andy Van Slyke doubled home two big runs for the Pirates in the seventh inning. Reds shortstop Barry Larkin and Bobby talked to each other during the game about how much fun the playoffs were. Both players were young superstars and could hardly contain their excitement.

The Reds took the second game of the series 2-1. The game was highlighted by a tremendous throw made by Cincinnati right-fielder Paul O'Neill in the sixth inning. He nailed Van Slyke at third base. The Reds took game three by a 6-3 score. The Pirates' two sluggers Bonilla and Bonds were unusually silent during the first few games of the series.

In the fourth game, the Reds were leading 4-3 when Bobby crushed a double into right-center field. He tried stretching it into a triple but got thrown out at third base by Eric Davis. The Reds won the game 5-3 to take a commanding lead in the series.

Pirate third baseman Jeff King could not play in the fifth game because he came down with a sore back. Leyland put Bobby at third, even though he had spent most of the season playing in right field. It turned out to be a great move.

The Pirates won the squeaker 3-2. Bobby saved the game when he turned a beautiful double play to kill a Reds rally. He ran in and grabbed a slow roller with his bare hand. He zipped the ball to second baseman Jose Lind, who made the relay to first baseman Sid Bream.

The Pirates lost the series when they dropped the next game 6-1.

That winter, Bobby wanted a big raise. He was one of the five best players in baseball and wanted to be paid like one. The Pirates were always known as a frugal franchise, and they did not want to part with the big money. They said no to giving Bobby a big contract. They took him to arbitration, where he was offered a $1.25 million contract. That may sound like a lot of money, but Bobby was actually being well underpaid when compared to other major-league players.

Bobby felt insulted. His personality began to change as he came to realize that sometimes baseball is a big business and not just a game.

CHAPTER 6
Bobby the Superstar

E ven though he was upset about his contract situation, he did not let it affect the way he played. Bobby was so dedicated that he hardly ever took a day off. He would play every single game.

"I gave Bobby a day off last year," said manager Jim Leyland. "And unless he's struggling in a big slump, I'm not going to give him another one. He drove me nuts sitting on the bench. He just wanted to get out there and play."

The Pirates got hot early in the season and never looked back. On April 27, Bobby collected three hits and four RBIs to lead the Pirates to a 10-1 romp over the rival New York Mets. They stayed in first place for the rest of the season.

"What do I have to do in Pittsburgh to make them want me to stay?" a frustrated Bobby would say during the season. He had made Pittsburgh his home and wanted to play there for his entire career. But he also wanted to get paid what he felt he was worth.

The Pirates cruised to another playoff berth. They clinched the National League East with a 2-1 win over the Phillies on September 22. They won 98 games and finished the season a whopping 14 games in front of the second place St. Louis Cardinals. Bobby had another great season, batting .302 with 18 home runs and 100 RBIs. He also hit 44 doubles. The Pirates were set to face the Atlanta Braves, who were known for having a great pitching staff.

Bobby laughed when reporters asked him if he felt pressure going up against the Braves' pitchers.

"You talk about pressure in baseball? Pressure is growing up in the South Bronx. We're talking about houses burning, people starving, and I'm supposed to be trembling because we're playing the Braves?" he said.

But once again, Bobby and Barry became nearly invisible during the Series.

The Pirates won the first game 5-1 but found themselves behind 1-0 in the ninth inning of game two. Bobby smacked a double in the bottom of the ninth against ace pitcher Steve Avery. But the other Pirate hitters could not bring him home, and the Bucs lost 1-0.

The Pirates lost game three but won game four. They also won game five, even though the Braves refused to give Bobby any good pitches to hit. They even walked him intentionally, twice.

But then all the Pirate bats went cold. They did not score another run in the Series. The Braves won game six 1-0 and took the clinching seventh game 4-0.

Those poor at-bats would be the last ones Bobby would take in a Pirate uniform. With his contract expired, Bobby was a free agent. That meant he could sign with whatever team he wanted to.

Leyland pleaded with Bobby to stay in Pittsburgh, and so did the fans. Even his wife, Millie, was not sure she wanted to leave her new home.

Bobby and his agent, Dennis Gilbert, set off to find the best deal possible. The teams that really wanted Bobby were the Philadelphia Phillies, the Chicago Cubs, the California Angels, and the New York Mets.

Even though the Angels pressed hard to get Bobby to sign with them, Bobby made it clear that he wanted to stay in the National League and on the East Coast so that he could be close to his family and friends. He told Dennis that he preferred to play for the Mets and asked him to make the deal. Pittsburgh entered the bidding war, but it was too little and too late.

On December 2, 1991, Bobby signed a five-year, $29 million contract with the New York Mets. He became the highest-paid athlete in all of sports, and he was playing for his hometown team. Millie could throw out the jewelry box filled with Shea Stadium infield dirt that Bobby had brought her so many years before. Shea Stadium was now his new home.

"I think people have enjoyed the way I play, and that's what I want them to enjoy," Bobby said after signing the contract. "Each year is different, but you want people to appreciate the way you play the game."

"New York City was in my heart," he said, explaining why he chose to play for the Mets. "I was born and raised there. The Mets showed an interest and I said this could be a lot of fun. It'll be hard to knock the smile off my face."

When Bobby signed with the Mets, he made it a point to get involved with local charities and children's organizations. He started visiting his old schools, and he saw how badly they all needed sports equipment. The kids were playing with worn, outdated gear.

Bobby decided to start the Bobby and Millie Bonilla Public School Fund. For every run that Bobby drove in, he would donate $500 to help provide sports equipment and increase athletic programs for students at I.S. 162, P.S. 77, and Lehman High School. He and Millie also donated money to Millie's old school, P.S. 72.

Bobby also went to the schools and spoke to the students. He urged them to stay in school and get a good education.

"Not everybody will become a baseball star," he told them. "Not everybody will be lucky enough to make the money that I am making. [You need to stay in school and get an education.]"

The 1992 New York Mets held a lot of promise. They had a great pitching staff and a solid lineup built around Bobby Bo's power and Vince Coleman's speed. Shea Stadium was sold out for Bobby's first game as a Met. The fans were happy to root for a player they had rooted against for so long.

The fans even cheered after Bobby struck out in his first Met at-bat, against St. Louis Cardinal pitcher

Jose DeLeon. Ironically, Bonilla had been traded for DeLeon earlier in his career, when the Pirates had acquired Bobby from the White Sox.

The cheers grew even louder when Bobby led off the fourth inning with a solo home run to right field, giving the Mets a 1-0 lead. He singled in the sixth inning with the Cardinals leading 2-1. Bobby struck out again in the eighth inning, but he would get another chance later in the game after the Mets tied the score 2-2 in the bottom of the ninth to force extra innings.

Bobby is congratulated at the plate by teammate Dave Magadan after hitting a 3-run home run against San Francisco, May 23, 1992.

Bobby came up in the tenth inning with Coleman on second base. A single would win the game because the speedy Coleman would surely score from second. Bobby turned on a hard slider from future Hall of Famer Lee Smith and drove it over the right-field wall. Bobby had won the game 4-2.

The Mets fans were ecstatic, but Bobby knew it was way too early to get very excited. "There are a lot more games to be played," he said.

He was right. After that first game, Bobby struggled mightily. Everything he did and said was scrutinized in the media. People began saying that he was not worth the money he was getting paid. Bobby was under a lot of pressure. He wanted to show that he was worth it.

He especially struggled at home games. By May 27, Bobby was only hitting .161 and the team, which was one of the highest-paid teams in baseball, was losing. By the end of May, the fans began to boo him. He got the fans to boo even louder when he told the media that he started to wear earplugs every time he came to bat. It was a season that Bobby would like to forget.

In mid-July, the previously mild-mannered Bobby got into a shouting match with Mets manager Jeff Torborg. But by August 2, the Mets still found themselves only 5 1/2 games behind the division-leading Pirates. That day would prove to be one of the worst days in team history.

Bobby was beginning to hit better and was starting to win some of the fans back. Howard Johnson hurt his wrist and star pitcher Bret Saberhagen was diagnosed with severe tendinitis in one of his pitching fingers. During the game, Bobby went into foul territory trying to catch a foul pop-up. He dove for the ball and ended up breaking a rib.

Bobby missed three weeks with his injury. By the time he was ready to play again, he found that the Mets had fallen way out of the pennant race. He belted four home runs in his first four games back after the injury, but it was too late. Two weeks later Bobby started complaining of a pain in his shoulder. The Mets' doctors examined him and decided that his shoulder required surgery. They decided to operate immediately so that Bobby would be back for the 1993 season.

Bobbby finished the season with his worst statistics up until that point. He batted .249 with 19 dingers and only 70 RBIs.

Bobby said that playing in New York was both frightening and exciting. He said he didn't mind being on that stage.

CHAPTER 7
Many Teams, One World Series

The next season, Bobby started off slowly for the Mets. But he continued to work hard. He even took batting practice after games. Bobby started tapping his baseball bat on his batting helmet after missing a pitch that he felt he should have hit. It is a habit he still has today.

Bobby did not endear himself to the fans or the sportswriters in New York, but the players all respected him. "For all the smiles that Bobby wears, he is never concerned with his image," said Mets teammate Dave Magadan. "Bobby plays hard, he protects the players and he does what it takes to win."

But Bobby continued to struggle in New York. He even nearly came to blows with New York sportswriter Bob Klapisch. In his book, Klapisch had called the Mets "the worst team that money can buy." He cited Bobby specifically in the book, and Bobby did not like it. After the incident, Bobby was constantly being shown in a bad light.

It did not help that the Mets, who had signed many expensive free agents, were playing like the worst team in baseball. The 1993 Mets was a team in shambles. With superstars like Bobby, Eddie Murray, Howard Johnson, Vince Coleman, Jeff Kent, Dwight Gooden, and John Franco, they were the most expensive last-place team in the history of baseball.

The team finished with the worst record in all of baseball, with an abominable 59-103 record. Bobby regained his home-run stroke, hitting 34 of them, but he batted only .265 with 87 RBIs. The team fired Torborg midway through the season and hired veteran manager Dallas Green.

Meanwhile, Barry Bonds was also forced to leave the Pittsburgh Pirates when they would not pay him his market value. Like Bobby, Bonds returned to his hometown, San Francisco. But, unlike Bobby, Bonds had a tremendous season under the pressure of a big contract. Barry batted .336 with 46 home runs and 123 RBIs. He lead the Giants to 103 victories.

The 1994 season was no better than 1993 for Bobby and the Mets. Bobby put up some decent numbers. but he was languishing on a terrible team. He started to get depressed from losing, and from losing every year.

By the 1995 season, Bobby's attitude had changed. He did not care anymore what the media wrote about him; he did not care whether the fans booed or not. Bobby started playing baseball because he loved the game. And it was no accident that he started the season off by playing some of his best baseball as a Met. It was Bobby's 10th major-league season. On May 12, against the Montreal Expos, Bobby hit home runs from both sides of the plate for the sixth time, a National League record.

By the middle of the season, it was clear once again that the Mets were going nowhere. Bobby was playing well, and several other teams were interested in trading for him for the playoff run.

After 80 games, Bobby was batting .325 with 18 home runs and 53 RBIs. The Baltimore Orioles, who were in second place, were very interested in adding Bobby's bat to their lineup. The Mets were interested in a young prospect that the Orioles had. And since the Mets had decided to rebuild, they decided to trade Bobby and end his experience in New York. They traded him and Jimmy Williams to Baltimore for prospect Alex Ochoa and veteran Damon Buford.

Bobby was rejuvenated playing for a good team. He was liked by Baltimore fans and responded by hitting .333 with 10 homers and 46 RBIs in 60 games for the Orioles. He appeared in his sixth All-Star Game and actually ended the season with a 20-game hitting streak, the third longest in Baltimore history. For the season, Bobby finished with a .329 average, 28 homers, and 99 RBIs, numbers that he was more accustomed to.

For the Orioles, Bobby proved valuable. He played first base, third base, left field, right field, and designated hitter. The Orioles came in second place, but with Bobby locked in for the 1996 season, they were looking forward to a real playoff push.

In 1996, Bobby had one of his best and most exciting seasons. After a slow start, which Bobby was

Bobby was rejuvenated playing for the Baltimore Orioles. In 1996, he had one of his best seasons.

now known for, he tore up the American League. After June 2, Bobby batted .346 with 25 home runs and

89 RBIs over 108 games. More importantly, he drove in more than 100 runs for the first time since 1991, when he was with the Pirates. Bobby was also driving in runs while making outs. He tied an American League record by making 17 sacrifice flies. A sacrifice fly is when a runner is able to score from third base after an outfielder catches a fly ball with less than two outs. Bobby also finished the season with 28 home runs, and the Orioles made the playoffs for the first time in years.

Bobby was going back to the playoffs. His only other appearances in the postseason had resulted in losses, with him playing particularly poorly. The Orioles faced off against the heavily favored Cleveland Indians, who were known as the powerhouse team of the American League.

The Orioles defeated the Indians in four games despite Bobby's hitting only .200. He did belt a couple of home runs in the series and drove in some key runs. Next up for the Orioles were their rivals, the New York Yankees.

The Yankees would beat the Orioles easily, sending Bobby home again without a World Series appearance. Against the Yanks, Bobby could not buy a hit. He finished the series with a pitiful .050 batting average. In nine playoff games, Bobby had hit three home runs and drove in seven runs. The Yankees went on to defeat the powerful Atlanta Braves in the World Series to become the champions.

Despite having a great season, Bobby was once again let down by his performance in the playoffs. That winter, he thought long and hard about what his next move would be. The mega-contract that he signed all those years before with the New York Mets had finally expired, and for the second time in his career, Bobby was a free agent.

Bobby liked the idea of playing for a contending team like Baltimore, but he had had a few run-ins during the season with manager Davey Johnson. But then something happened that helped Bobby make up his mind. His old friend and former manager, Jim

Bobby enjoyed playing for the pennant-contending team, the Baltimore Orioles, but he had a few run-ins during the season with manager Davey Johnson.

Leyland, was now the manager of the National League's Florida Marlins. He called Bobby up after the season and told him that he should come to Florida. That November, Bobby signed a contract making him a Marlin. He joined a powerful team that featured home-run hitter Gary Sheffield, All-Star Moises Alou, hard-hitting infielder Kevin Conine, and star pitchers Kevin Brown and Livian Hernandez. As the season got under way, the Marlins were clearly one of the teams to beat in the National League. But there was no way that the Marlins were going to finish in front of the perennial National League champion Atlanta Braves. They had too much of a pitching staff with Greg Maddux, John Smoltz, and Tom Glavine.

The Marlins actually battled the upstart New York Mets for the wild-card playoff spot all season. Bobby's season was filled with career landmarks. On June 9 in San Francisco, Bobby drove in his 1,000th career run. He established a Florida Marlins record by pounding 39 doubles. He batted .297 with 17 homers and 96 RBIs. His 17 round-trippers moved him past Ken Singleton and Ted Simmons and into fifth place on the all-time list for home runs by a switch-hitter. Bobby now had 262 career home runs. Other highlights for Bobby included a league-leading three grand slams and a pair of ten-game hitting streaks. He also belted a monstrous 495-foot home run during a winning game against the Detroit Tigers.

The Marlins faced off against the San Francisco Giants in the first round of the playoffs. They swept the Giants. The Marlins pitchers had their game faces on when they upstaged the Braves during the NLCS. Rookie Livan Hernandez struck out 15 batters in Game 5 in front of a cheering crowd of 51,982 at Pro Player Stadium in Miami. Ace Kevin Brown, battling a stomach ailment, then pitched a complete game in Game 6 to send Florida into the World Series. It was Bobby's first appearance, and he would not be denied.

The Series took seven games to settle the outcome. Bobby played his heart out, even with the tough hamstring injury, and was inspirational to his teammates and the fans. He even had a few clutch hits and a big home run in the Series. Before the Marlins took the field for Game 7, Leyland gathered the players in the clubhouse. "Next time we're in this room," he told the team, "we'll be world champions."

Because the Marlins were an expansion team, started only in 1993, no one expected them to do well. Expansion teams need time to develop their players, so their National League Championship was a surprise to many. They were not favored to win the World Series. But the team pulled together and did it. Bobby was finally a World Series winner. It was a moment that Bobby and his friend Leyland had waited for their whole lives. They savored their special moment together.

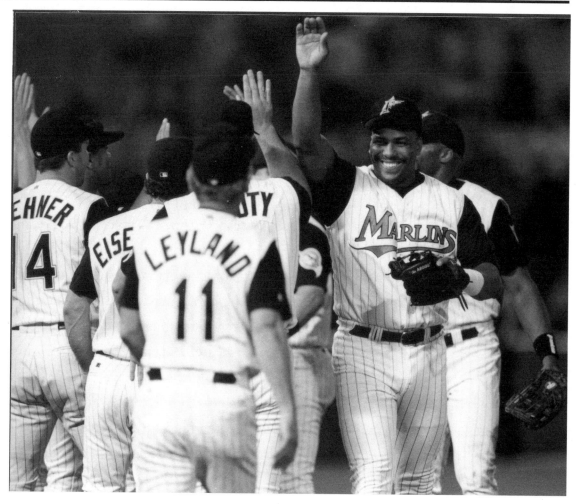

"It's special for all of our players," Leyland said, "but privately, Bobby and I have a different feeling about making it. We know how we both feel about the situation. It's something that maybe the other players can't share."

Bobby was well liked in Florida. He got along well with the media and got involved in a lot of charitable work in the Florida area. But, unfortunately, he was not able to enjoy his World Series victory for long.

The 1997 Marlins celebrated their win of the World Series. They could not celebrate very long, however. Shortly after their victory, the owners began breaking up the team.

The Florida Marlins were experiencing serious financial troubles. The owners of the team were determined to cut the team's payroll. They spent the off-season trading away most of their stars. They got rid of Moises Alou, Conine, Brown, closer Rob Nenn, and pitchers Al Leiter and Dennis Cook.

Bobby remained with the team through the start of the 1998 season, but it seemed only a matter of time before he would be traded, too. He started the season with the Marlins on the disabled list. He was still recovering from off-season surgery on his left wrist and left Achilles' tendon. Then, on May 12, the Marlins traded Bobby, Jim Eisenreich, Gary Sheffield, and minor-league pitcher Manuel Barrios, along with outstanding catcher Charles Johnson, to the Los Angeles Dodgers for superstar catcher Mike Piazza and infielder Todd Zeile. Marlin fans couldn't even get used to cheering for Piazza. He was traded a week later to the New York Mets for some inexperienced, and inexpensive, minor-league players.

Bobby was with his sixth team, but he was used to the traveling. And now that he had won his World Series, he didn't care which team he played for. He just wanted to get back and win another world championship.

Unfortunately, the 1998 season was not a good one for Bobby. During the season he was on the disabled list from June 18 through July 2 with an intestinal infection after having a non-cancerous growth re-

Bobby signs autographs for his adoring fans.

moved near his colon, and again from July 15 through August 4 with left wrist tendinitis. To make matters worse, at the end of the season, the Dodgers announced that they had hired Davey Johnson to be their new manager after Felipe Alou of the Montreal Expos turned down their offer. Bobby had played for Davey when he was with the Mets and again with the Orioles. The two did not get along well.

On Thursday, November 12, 1998, Bobby was traded again—back home to the New York Mets, in exchange for right-handed pitcher Mel Rojas.

"Bobby lends another big bat to our line-up to supplement John Olerud and Mike Piazza," said Mets interim general manager Frank Cashen. "Last year was a tough year for Bobby with all of the injuries, but we are confident that he is healthy and will help our team."

Between his injuries and medical problems, 1998 was not a good year for Bobby.

"Bobby's presence in the line-up gives Mike Piazza excellent protection," added Mets manager Bobby Valentine.

"I'm thrilled to be back in New York and back home," said Bonilla. "I was fortunate enough to win a World Series with the Marlins, but my ultimate goal has always been to bring a world championship back to the Mets." In the business of baseball, there aren't always multiple choices. Bobby is a versatile player and he has adapted to the constant changes.

In describing Bobby Bonilla, Jim Leyland says it best:

"Two things sum up Bobby Bonilla: he enjoys life and he enjoys baseball. And that's a pretty nice combination."

Back in a Mets uniform, Bobby Bonilla looks forward to the rest of his baseball career.

MAJOR LEAGUE STATS

YR	TEAM	G	AB	R	H	2B	3B	HR	RBI	BB	AVG
1986	2TM	138	426	55	109	16	4	3	43	62	.256
	ChA	75	234	27	63	10	2	2	26	33	.269
	Pit	63	192	28	46	6	2	1	17	29	.240
1987	Pit	141	466	58	140	33	3	15	77	39	.300
1988	Pit	159	584	87	160	32	7	24	100	85	.274
1989	Pit	163	616	96	173	37	10	24	86	76	.281
1990	Pit	160	625	112	175	39	7	32	120	45	.280
1991	Pit	157	577	102	174	44	6	18	100	90	.302
1992	NYN	128	438	62	109	23	0	19	70	66	.249
1993	NYN	139	502	81	133	21	3	34	87	72	.265
1994	NYN	108	403	60	117	24	1	20	67	55	.290
1995	2TM	141	554	96	182	37	8	28	99	54	.329
	NYN	80	317	49	103	25	4	18	53	31	.325
	Bal	61	237	47	79	12	4	10	46	23	.333
1996	Bal	159	595	107	171	27	5	28	116	75	.287
1997	Fla	153	562	77	167	39	3	17	96	73	.297
1998	2TM	100	333	39	83	11	1	11	45	41	.249
	Fla	28	97	11	27	5	0	4	15	12	.278
	LA	72	236	28	56	6	1	7	30	29	.237
TOTALS		1846	6681	1032	1893	383	58	273	1106	833	.283

CHRONOLOGY

1963	Born February 23
1981	Played in Europe on Amateur Team in June; signed by the Pittsburgh Pirates as a free agent on July 11
1985	Selected by the Chicago White Sox as a Rule V free agent in December
1986	Traded back to the Pirates on July 23
1988	Named to the Sporting News Hillerich and Bradsby Silver Slugger Team; Bobby and Millie's daughter, Danielle, born on December 16
1990	Led the National League with 78 extra-base hits; finished second to teammate Barry Bonds in the Most Valuable Player voting; named to the Sporting News Hillerich and Bradsby Silver Slugger Team
1991	Named to the Sporting News Hillerich and Bradsby Silver Slugger Team; signed with the New York Mets as a free agent on December 2
1993	Bobby and Millie's son, Brandon Ace, born on October 21
1995	Traded to the Baltimore Orioles on July 28
1996	Tied American League record of 17 sacrifice flies; signed with the Florida Marlins in December
1997	Led the National League with three grand slams; established a Marlins record by hitting 39 doubles; won his first World Series after hitting dramatic game-tying home run; traded to the Los Angeles Dodgers in a package for catcher Mike Piazza
1998	On disabled list most of the season; November 12, traded to the New York Mets

INDEX